Salt & Pepper

Shakers

IDENTIFICATION & VALUES

Helene Guarnaccia

Photography by Michael La Chioma

COLLECTOR BOOKS
A Division of Schroeder Publishing Co., Inc.

The current values in this book should be used only as guide. They are not intended to set prices, which vary from one section of the country to another. Auction prices as well as dealer prices vary greatly and are affected by condition as well as demand. Neither the Author nor the Publisher assumes responsibility for any losses that might be incurred as a result of consulting this guide.

Searching For A Publisher?

We are always looking for knowledgeable people considered to be experts within their fields. If you feel that there is a real need for a book on your collectible subject and have a large comprehensive collection, contact Collector Books.

Collector Books
P.O. Box 3009
Paducah, KY 42002-3009

Copyright © 1985 by Helene Guarnaccia

All rights reserved. No part of this book may be reproduced, stored in any retrieval system, or transmitted in any form, or by any means including but not limited to electronic, mechanical, photocopy, recording, or otherwise, without the written consent of the author and publisher.

Printed by IMAGE GRAPHICS, INC., Paducah, Kentucky.

Dedication

To my sons Peter and Steven. Steven, who gave me two pairs of salt and pepper shakers three years ago, started this whole thing! He has long been a creative influence in my life, and has opened up many new avenues of interests. Being with him is always an adventure and a joy.

Peter recently found me a collection of two hundred pairs of salt and pepper shakers–the impetus for this second book. With his wife Linda, he hand wrapped and delivered four hundred individual shakers–truly a labor of love. Peter is always there when I need him; someone I can always count on for guidance and support.

And to my parents, Essie and Ted Sulzer, who brought me up to believe that all things are possible. I thank them for making me feel capable and important. Their influence on my life is beyond measure.

Acknowledgments

I would like to thank the following people for allowing me to borrow from their private collections to have photographs taken for this book. I appreciate how precious ones' own collection is, and I am very grateful for the trust and consideration shown to me by so many people.

Barbara A. Gilmore, Barbara's Barn Antiques, Ridgefield, CT
Robin Kinney, Fairfield, CT
Dawn and Bob La Ganza
Ron and Alice Lindholm, Treasure Seekers, New York City
Bob Manley, South Easton, MA
Barbara Stevens, Stratford, CT
Bonnie Loffay, Pougkeepsie, NY
Rene Malin, Wisconsin Rapids; photographs from her collection include the pig and the Mexican nodders, the three chefs, the Mercedes racing cars and the old wooden cars. They were photographed by Dale E. Bowden.
A kind friend from Long Island who chooses to remain anonymous.
"The 38 United Stated of America" was assembled by Professor John Fawcett of the University of Connecticut. This collage is from the collection of Lynn and Noel Barrett, proprietors of Rosebud Antiques of Carversville, PA. Thanks to Mr. Barrett for taking the photograph and for allowing me to use it in this book.

And once again, a very special thanks to photographer par excellence, Michael La Chioma. His unfailing patience and consistent good humor made a difficult job a pleasure.

Table of Contents

Introduction

Since my first book on salt and pepper shakers described the history and uses of salt and the development of the shaker from open salt dishes, there seems little need to repeat; the history of salt has not changed.

I would like, instead, to mention some of the interesting letters I have received since the first book was published. I found particularly fascinating the tremendous variety of shakers that people collect. I have received wonderful mail and would like to share some of the anecdotes relating to reader's collections.

A woman from Colorado wrote that she furnishes and decorates doll houses with salt and pepper shaker furniture. There are television sets and refrigerators, washers and dryers, people in rocking chairs, sofas and beds: what a novel idea!

Another collector in Pennsylvania has limited her collection to water-related sets. She started with fish and water birds: penguins, flamingos, swans, ducks, pelicans, etc. Her collection expanded to include sprinkling cans, water pumps, boats, mermaids, umbrellas, shellfish and fishermen, and a lady in a bath tub! What a fun collection. I got so interested in it that I found a deep sea diver with two fish, Niagra Falls, and hot water bottle with a pair of feet!

I have heard from collectors who collect only advertising sets, an antique dealer who collects only plastic sets that move, like the piano, the toaster, and the lawn mower; another dealer who collects only sets whose shakers are actually the shape of the thing depicted, like the bowling pins, thermos bottles and irons.

There is a New York couple who haunts flea markets looking for comic characters and personality sets; they have a marvelous collection including Orphan Annie, Popeye and Olive Oyl, Dick Tracy, Charlie McCarthy, and Laurel and Hardy, to name a few.

I met an advertising executive who collects, of course, advertising salt and pepper shakers and plastic ones too. He suggested photographing the shakers in their "natural habitat"–the power mower, for example, in the grass, cutting a tiny strip first with scissors so that it would appear that the mower had done the job! Truly a creative mind at work.

I have found the different kinds of sets people collect to be fascinating, and the size and scope of their collections to be awe-inspiring. A correspondent from Wisconsin has almost 6,000 pairs, one of her specialties being nodders. She hopes to see them all displayed in one space some day soon, by having shelves built all around a 40 ft. long cellar. She is only 27 years old, has been collecting for 10 years, and also races stock cars.

Someone I met from Massachusetts collects only sets that have matching mustard jars, a man from California collects souvenir sets, and another collector specializes in miniatures. A Connecticut couple, near neighbors, are both avid collectors. He collects nodders and she collects Occupied Japan. Another Connecticut collector collected salt and pepper shakers in the shape of fruits and vegetables and put them in a pewter bowl in the middle of her dining room table for a unique centerpiece.

A Salt and Pepper Shaker Club exists whose members collect both the novelty type, and the antique glass type which are truly beautiful. They publish a newletter, and offer a column which acts as a clearing house for buying, selling and exchanging. For more information or for an application for membership, write to Dottie and Bill Avery, 2832 Rapidan Trail, Maitland, Florida 32751.

I have thoroughly enjoyed the mail that I have received. There is certainly a bond among collectors: we all enjoy the hunt, the pursuit, and most of all the wonderful find–truly a case where the end justifies the means.

Advertising and Promotion

Aunt Jemima and Uncle Mose, red plastic; black and white flashed on. Paint comes off easily; do not wash! Came in two sizes: 3½" $28.00-32.00. Large size 5" $40.00-45.00. There is a matching cookie jar, syrup pitchers, and a complete spice set. Planters Peanuts, plastic. The tan and black pictured is the original color. $18.00-22.00 pr. Also came in other colors: red, green and gold.

Tappan Range Chefs, ceramic. $10.00-15.00. Westinghouse washer and dryer, plastic, 1950. $20.00-25.00.

Tappan chefs, plastic. $8.00-10.00.

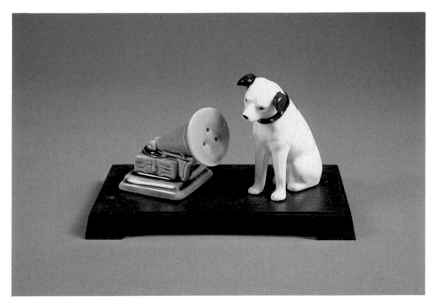

RCA Corporation *"Nipper,"* new, authorized by RCA. Older ones made by Lenox and in Japan. These are also Japanese. $22.00-25.00.

General Electric refrigerators. Salt, pepper and sugar bowl. Salt and pepper have metal top; sugar bowl top is same white milk glass as rest of set. Salt and pepper alone. $30.00-35.00: with G.E stickers $40.00-45.00. Three-piece set as shown. $100.00-125.00.

World's Fair, New York 1939, orange and blue plastic (I have another pair with the color reversed). $25.00-28.00. World's Fair, New York 1965, blue and white plastic. $12.00-15.00. Emeloid Co., Arlington, NJ.

Ken-L-Ration dog and cat, F&F plastic, U.S.A. $12.00-15.00. With matching
creamer and sugar, $35.00-40.00 for four-piece set. Willie and Millie penguins,
1933. To introduce Kool cigarettes. Also made by F&F plastics. $12.00-15.00.

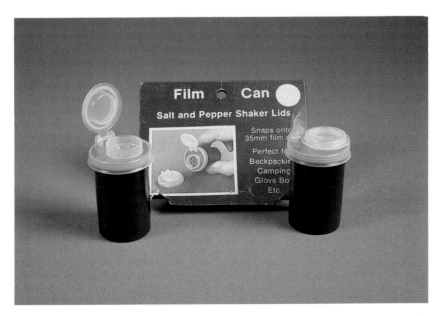

Film canisters, a solution for what to do with them all! Now you can buy salt
and pepper tops for $2.00 to convert them into waterproof, airtight shakers.
Made by Hall Brothers, Morgan, UT.

Italian Swiss Colony Chianti wine, glass and straw. These are very common. $4.00-6.00. Lancers White and Rose wines, salt and pepper tops (plastic) offered as a promotion to go on individual bottles. $6.00-8.00.

Big Boy, a restaurant chain, ceramic. $200.00-225.00. Safe-T-Cup ice cream cones, ceramic, $18.00-22.00.

Vess soda, a "billion bubble beverage," glass. $8.00-10.00.

Budweiser beer, glass bottle with paper label. $6.00-10.00. Twisted neck Chianti bottle, glass and straw. $3.00-5.00.

Sheraton Hotel Bellhop. Made by Goebel. This set was designed by Zetz-
mann, a sculptor, in 1953. It was part of a line of sugars and creamers, and
the salt and pepper set retailed for $24.00. The salt and pepper are the suit-
cases, and they have real leather handles. $150.00-175.00. (Information cour-
tesy of the Goebel Museum in Tarryton, NY.)

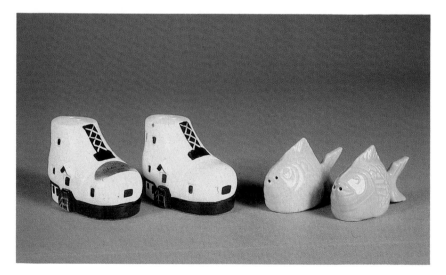

The Shoe House, York, PA, ceramic. $4.00-6.00. Fish, "Chicken of the Sea,"
ceramic. $6.00-8.00.

Pillsbury "Poppin Fresh," ceramic. $8.00-10.00. Guckenheimer Whiskey, glass bottles. $6.00-8.00.

Plastic gas pumps, Esso, Gulf, and Mobil. Besides advertising the gasoline company, these often caried the name of the service station printed on the back. $20.00-22.00.

More glass bottles: Piels Real Draft Beer. $4.00-6.00. Old Stagg Bourbon. $5.00-8.00. Sealtest Milk Bottles (even real milk doesn't come in a glass bottles anymore!) $20.00-22.00.

Utica Club Brewery, replica of old steins. Utica Club took these as their logo in 1959. Webco–West End Brewery Co. The originals were made in Germany, then in Brazil, now in Germany again. The large figure is Schultz, and the small one is Dooley. There were also ice buckets and beer steins; this set is marked Ceramarte Ltda., Rio Negrino, made in Brazil, Webco. $35.00-45.00. Blatz beer $8.00-10.00.

Animals

Black Cats. The long thin cat is salt and pepper in one. It has two corks, on at each end. $8.00-10.00. The small sitting pair are not the Shafford cats; they have white instead of green eyes. $5.00-7.00. The third pair of cats have rhinestone eyes! $12.00-15.00.

This little black cat is looking into a ceramic gold fish bowl. $10.00-15.00. These green-eyed, pink-eared cats hold gold fish bowls filled with real water and tiny plastic fish. These are truly wonderful, and the only pair like them that I have seen. $110.00-135.00.

More cats, the center are the Stafford cats. There is a whole line of this pottery, including teapots, creamer and sugar, ash trays, measuring cups, etc. $15.00-18.00. White cats trimmed in blue; a little sad looking. $8.00-10.00.

Luster cats, quite aristocratic. $12.00-15.00. These ceramic cats are on, instead of behind the eight ball. $10.00-12.00.

Cartoon type ceramic animals; the dogs look sewn like stuffed animals; there are many other animals like this. The cats are striped. $5.00-7.00.

A pair of cartoon dogs, ceramic. $8.00-10.00. Dog and hydrant, a common theme; this hydrant has a metal chain. $8.00-10.00.

Two pairs of ceramic dogs, dalmations and bull dogs. $8.00-10.00.

Two dogs playing. $6.00-8.00. The gingham dog and the calico cat. $12.00-15.00.

The sad eyed dogs on the left say "I'm salt" and "I'm pep" on their tags. $8.00-10.00. The dogs in the center look planed, almost as though carved. I have seen elephants and ducks like this and also toothpick holders. $7.00-9.00. The Bonzo dogs on the right are patterned after the Bonzo cartoon dog; this pair is chalk-like composition. $10.00-12.00.

Ceramic dogs. $4.00-6.00. This pair of Bonzo dogs has shiny gold paws and is high gloss ceramic. $12.00-15.00.

A pair of white ceramic poodles, trimmed with "gingerbread." $12.00-15.00.
The dachsund is split; one half salt and one half pepper (total length 7").
$8.00-10.00.

A large split dachsund (each half measures 5"). $8.00-10.00.

Black ceramic French poodles. $8.00-10.00. Ceramic Boston bulls, each bandaged over one eye. $18.00-20.00.

A schnauzer in a hat? $8.00-10.00. Hugging dogs. These are seated and sweet. $8.00-10.00.

A pair of monkeys, 3" tall. $8.00-10.00. A wonderful kangaroo with baby–the mother is salt, the baby, pepper. These are well sculpted. $18.00-22.00.

Two pairs of kangaroos: The brown kangaroo with baby is 4" tall. $15.00-18.00. The blue and white ones are very large (6" tall) and unrealistic looking. $10.00-15.00.

The mother and baby bear are part of a whole series of animals whose young are seated on their laps. $24.00-28.00. The fawn are Occupied Japan. $10.00-12.00.

Two more "Mother and Baby" sets: dogs and turtles. $6.00-8.00.

Puss 'N Boots. $25.00-35.00. Shawnee Pig shakers. $25.00-35.00.

Muggsy dog and Shawnee Farmer pig. $25.00-35.00 pair.

*Shawnee Pottery began in Zanesville, Ohio in 1937, and closed in 1961. The company's first designer, Rudy Ganz, was from Germany. He designed the pigs and Puss 'N Boots and worked for Shawnee from 1939-1954.

*Shawnee Pottery, Dolores Simon, Collector Books, 1977.

Turtles and alligators–both ceramic and both made in Japan as are most of the animals pictured here. $6.00-8.00.

There are various sets of these beetles; one of these is holding a broken heart. $8.00-10.00. Turtles with umbrellas. $6.00-8.00.

Black high gloss elephants and an elephant on a stand. $5.00-7.00. One collector I met put together a whole circus using shakers such as these.

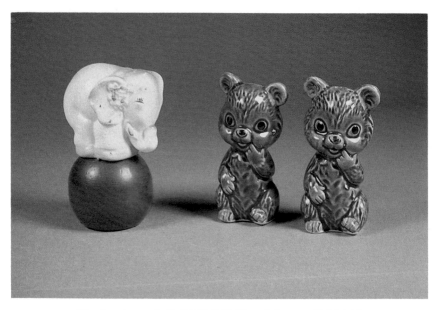

Elephant on a ball. $6.00-8.00. Purple bears. $2.00-4.00.

More elephants: the smaller ones are "Dumbo." $22.00-24.00. Large set $8.00-10.00.

Monkeys and giraffes. Ceramic. $10.00-12.00.

The brown monkeys are not as clearly delineated. $4.00-6.00. The monkey on the ball is marked Shafford, Japan. It appears to be from the 1940's and is nicely detailed. The ball is the salt; the monkey the pepper. $20.00-22.00.

These two pairs of monkeys are again the cartoon type, not meant to be realistic. First pair, $4.00-6.00. Second pair, $6.00-8.00. The monkey and the cello is a unique set. $15.00-18.00.

There are many variations of the mouse with the cheese. The smaller set is
intricately designed so that the mouse fits in the cheese. $15.00-18.00. The
larger set says "chunky." $12.00-15.00.

The chipmunks are cartoon type figures. $4.00-6.00. The white rabbits are a
high glaze ceramic. $6.00-8.00.

Animals dressed in clothes seem to be a take-off of a children's book illustration; these two pairs are cute. Skunks. $5.00-7.00. Mice. $8.00-10.00.

The dogs are basset hounds. The skunks are silly, but collectible. Basset hounds. $8.00-10.00. Skunks. $6.00-8.00.

These foxes are very realistic and nicely colored and designed. The glaze is excellent. Relco, Japan. $12.00-15.00.

Playful fawns. $6.00-8.00. A fawn with fur; this can't really have been meant to hold salt! $3.00-5.00.

Cows–now a popular "country kitchen" item. The blue and white cows are reminiscent of the old cow creamers. $8.00-10.00. The heads are bells as well as salt and pepper shakers. $10.00-12.00.

Donkeys and lambs; ceramic. $6.00-8.00.

The bright yellow pigs are chalk and have some age. $6.00-8.00. The pale yellow pigs are high gloss ceramic. $4.00-5.00.

The roosters are old; they belonged to a friend's grandmother. They have an interesting texture and a matte glaze. $15.00-18.00. Hampshire sow and boar. When I saw these I thought they were the figment of some artist's imagination, but they are authentic Hampshire pigs. An almost identical picture is in the *Encyclopedia Britannica*. These pigs originated in England and were later introduced in the United States. The salt and pepper shakers are of a beautiful quality porcelain; unfortunately they are not marked. They look like German or English fine china. They are well crafted, have wonderful faces, and the sow is clearly distinguishable from the boar. $28.00-32.00.

The bear with the garbage pail is 5" tall, and the dressed up bears are 3" tall. All are ceramic. Bear with pail. $8.00-10.00. Dressed up bears. $12.00-15.00.

The camel is 4½" tall. The two sacks which slip onto hooks are the salt and pepper. $8.00-10.00. The cigarettes and matches say "Gold Fold" a take-off, of course, of a popular brand. $8.00-10.00.

The owls are 2" tall. $5.00-7.00. These tiny bears are 1½" tall. $5.00-7.00.

Steer and donkeys (steer souvenir of Gettysburg, PA). $5.00-7.00.

These English bulls in the barrel have a wood-grained look, but they are ceramic. $6.00-8.00. One of these beetles is carrying what looks like a magnifying glass; he could be Dr. Watson. The other may be a doctor come to mend the broken heart of the beetle on page 27. $8.00-10.00.

Birds, Fish and Fowl

The cardinals are fairly realistic, high gloss glaze. $8.00-10.00. Kenmar, Japan. These green and yellow birds are 4½" tall; they have a noise box inside, so that when you turn over the salt they "sing." $8.00-10.00.

The yellow and black birds are fairly common. $4.00-6.00. The two little birds in the tray are luster and very charming. $12.00-15.00.

The orange and blue birds are Occupied Japan. $8.00-10.00. The small gray and brown birds are an unusual color. $10.00-12.00.

Two pairs of owls; the ones that are both tan have "googly eyes" that move. $8.00-10.00 per pair.

These quail are nicely colored and realistic. $10.00-12.00. These broad billed
shakers are rather charming. $10.00-12.00.

The swans are Occupied Japan. $10.00-12.00. These parrots are very colorful.
$10.00-12.00.

The red-headed woodpeckers are nicely crafted; one fits under the wing of the other. $12.00-15.00.

The two hugging penguins are of a dull glaze. $12.00-15.00. The wooden wheelbarrow holds two wooden penguins. $8.00-10.00.

The small blue penguins are among my favorites. $12.00-15.00. The larger penguins have red noses and appear to be a little tipsy! $12.00-15.00.

Ring-necked pheasant–easily indentified. $8.00-10.00. Wild turkeys. $8.00-10.00.

White swans proclaim "together always." $6.00-8.00. Pink tinged swans. $6.00-8.00.

The geese with their necks bent are Occupied Japan. $10.00-14.00. The ducks are of a high-gloss pottery. $6.00-8.00.

Cartoon type birds all dressed up. $6.00-8.00. Birds sitting in a nest. $8.00-10.00.

The bird and the nest are the salt and pepper shakers. They both have notches that fit into holes in the branch. $12.00-15.00. Brightly colored exotic birds. $8.00-10.00.

Pelicans, both ceramic and both made in Japan. $8.00-10.00.

Flamingos come in many poses and are highly collectible. $15.00-18.00.

Brightly colored fish, also very collectible. $8.00-10.00.

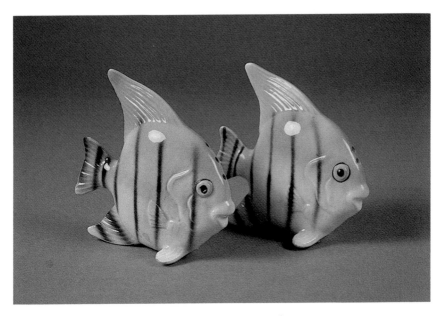

Tropical fish, glossy finish; 4½". $8.00-10.00.

Heavy silvery metal and two pairs of ceramic fish. $10.00-12.00.

Ceramic fish, are all made in Japan. $8.00-10.00.

More Fish. $8.00-10.00.

The seals without the ball have whiskers. Those balancing a ball could be part of a circus. $8.00-10.00 pair.

Whales. The single whale should be paired with a black boy. Single shaker. $18.00-22.00. Whale with black boy. $45.00-65.00. Larger whales. $6.00-8.00.

With the popularity of country kitchens, both cows and chickens have become highly collectible. $8.00-10.00.

These small chicken sets are very popular. $6.00-8.00.

The white chickens are unusually large–4" tall. $8.00-10.00. The chickens "feeding" are less common than some. $6.00-9.00.

More chickens; one holding a golden egg. $6.00-8.00.

The half white and half red pair of chickens are poorly colored. $6.00-8.00.
The black and white chickens look to be from the 40's; they have nice detail.
$12.00-15.00.

Two baby birds in a nest. $8.00-10.00. The chicken and rooster are sitting on a tray of eggs. $10.00-12.00.

Both pairs of these yellow chicks are older than most of the other chicken sets. Chicks with many large holes in head (perhaps salt was coarser then). $8.00-10.00. Pair in shell with holder. $10.00-12.00.

Large brown turkeys. $5.00-7.00. Turkeys on a tray, brightly colored. $8.00-10.00.

Nice realistic pair of turkeys. $6.00-8.00. Large bisque-type turkeys trimmed in gold. $4.00-6.00.

"Jailbirds" made by Fitz and Floyd, 1980, sure to become collectible! The cage is metal. $35.00-50.00.

Black Americana

This "family" consists of six pieces; the tallest are 8" tall salt and pepper shakers. $100.00-125.00. The four figures on the tray are 5" oil and vinegar cruets, and 3½" salt and peppers. $125.00-150.00.

The vinegar and oil cruets have removable hands with attached corks for stoppers. The salt and pepper shakers match. The complete set, $110.00-125.00.

Mammys and Chefs; these are quite common. $15.00 each. $35.00-45.00 pair.

The small pearl china set is unusual. $30.00-40.00. The set marked "salty" and "peppy" is 4 ½" tall. $60.00-75.00.

The bisque figures are African dancers. $15.00-25.00. The seated figures appear to have been holding something in their laps, probably watermelons. $20.00-25.00. Set made by Goebel. $40.00-45.00.

Two children playing in a basket, high gloss glaze. $40.00-45.00.

Wooden chefs. $10.00-15.00. "Book" salt and pepper set. $15.00-20.00.

Fat cook and Mammy. $45.00-50.00. Large Mammy and Chef heads, 5½" tall. $50.00-60.00.

Head with watermelon. $40.00-45.00. Very beautiful bisque heads, these are rare. There are three on tray, middle is mustard (not shown). $75.00-85.00. Condiment set $200.00+.

Tall man and woman. $60.00-75.00. Fat cook and Mammy. $35.00-45.00.

Caricature figures with watermelon. $35.00-40.00.

Black heads. $15.00-20.00. Black clown teapots. There is a large teapot that matches these; probably a creamer and sugar as well. I have seen the same clown teapot salt and pepper shakers with white faces. There is another black clown series with red and green hats instead of the yellow straw type. $15.00-20.00.

Little Black Sambo and the Tiger. This is a beautiful and hard-to-find set. The figures are well crafted and nicely glazed. $150.00-200.00. Palm tree and seated black man. $30.00-35.00.

Small chalkware figures (don't put price stickers on these; the paint will come off with the sticker). $25.00-35.00. A kissing couple. $25.00-30.00.

Mammy with salt, pepper, and mustard on a tray. $40.00-50.00.

Eastern blacks with turbans. $18.00-24.00. Black African dancers, these are not really "Americana." $18.00-24.00.

Pearl China Co. "Peppy" and "Salty" dressed in yellow. These come in many colors-aqua, black, red, etc. $60.00-75.00. Mammy carrying two canisters (3 pieces). $55.00-65.00.

Black butler holding two bottles (the salt and pepper), 1920's. Marked on bottom: "Hand decorated Tric China Nagoya-Japan." $150.00-200.00.

Boxed Sets

Finding a collectible in its original box increases its value. The box may give information as to date, name of manufacturer, or country of origin. For example, many of the boxes stamped "Occupied Japan" have contents which are only marked "Japan." At the very least, objects found in their original boxes are much more apt to be in mint condition, as are the salt and pepper shakers that follow.

Tiny croquet salt and pepper set and steak markers. The salt and peppers are the mallets, the "balls" are marbles. The wickets are the steak markers marked rare, medium, and well-done! With box, as shown $30.00. Without box $20.00-25.00.

Light bulbs. These come in clear glass in amber, cobalt blue and amethyst. In opaque glass they also come in a variety of colors. These were made for Chadwick-Miller, Inc. of Boston, in Japan, copyright 1970. $8.00-10.00.

Coffee Pots on a balcony with a canopy and the New York City skyline in the background. The back of the package says "Penthouse, Brillium Metals Corp., L.I.C., N.Y.-the excitement of Penthouse living, the glamour of dinner at The Ritz will be yours when you add these authentic miniatures to your table setting." All that from owning a pair of plastic salt and pepper shakers! In box $15.00. Without box $8.00-10.00.

Coffee Pots with burner; iridescent paper on the coils makes it look as though the burners are lit. Coffee pots are glass; hot plate is metal. $15.00.

Umbrella stands, unbrellas are the shakers (note S&P on handles). These come in bright red and other colors. $10.00. Salt 'N Pepper hat rack, made in U.S. Toothpick holder in base; black derby and yellow straw hat are the shakers. All plastic. With box $15.00. Without box $10.00.

Book rack by Davis. The two "books" on either end of set are the salt and pepper shakers; the middle "books" are attached, have a lift-off lid and form a sugar container. $10.00-15.00.

The horse and buggy set is made of wood. $8.00-10.00.

Lawn Mower. This tiny power mower has cylinders that move up and down as you push it. $10.00-15.00.

Dream House salt and pepper set and napkin holder. The two shrubs in front of the house are the shakers. $10.00-15.00. With box $20.00.

Flower Cart. Metal, glass salt and pepper shakers. Center holder with flowers may also be used for toothpicks. $10.00-15.00.

Miniature Mixer, plastic. The beaters are the salt and peppers. The removable bowl is a sugar bowl. $15.00-20.00.

Plastic television set. This can double as a snapshot holder by depressing the screen and inserting a photo. The salt and pepper shakers are in the top of the set, and pop up when the T.V. knob is turned. $15.00-20.00.

Li'l Washer is plastic, the wringers are the salt and pepper, the washer base says "sugar." $10.00-15.00. With box $20.00.

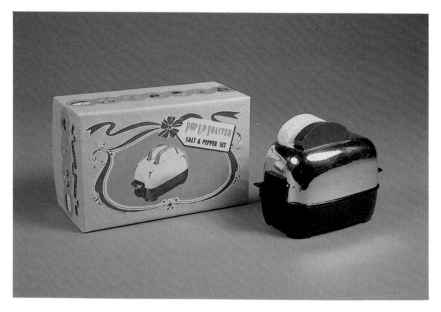

Toaster, a Starke Design. The brown "slice" is pepper, the white is salt. They pop up when the lever is pushed down. $10.00-15.00. With box $20.00.

Old fashioned car. The people are the removable salt and pepper shakers. $10.00-15.00. With box $20.00.

Melody music notes on a metal bar. The notes come off the stand and are the salt and peppers. This set is plastic and metal and is made in the U.S. $10.00-15.00. With box $20.00.

Gold and white plastic piano; press the keys and the salt and pepper pop up at the top of the piano. $10.00-15.00. With box $20.00.

Christmas Sets

Candles with choir girl, white ceramic. $6.00-8.00. Praying children, ceramic. $6.00-8.00.

Cartoon animals with Santa hats. $5.00-7.00 pair.

Candy cane figures, ceramic. $10.00-15.00. Stylized Santas with an "emerald" eye! $10.00-15.00.

Angels with red poinsettia hats, ceramic. $10.00-15.00. Christmas Bells. $5.00-7.00.

Santa Claus heads. These come in many sizes and designs; they are of high gloss ceramic. $8.00-10.00.

Full figure Santas also come in a variety of shapes and sizes. $10.00-12.00.

The Christmas boat; the flag says "Noel." The figures are removable and are the salt and pepper, the "smokestack" is a mustard pot. Holt Howard, 1950's. $35.00-45.00.

Mr. and Mrs. Santa. The pair with the gold trim appears to be older than some of the others. $12.00-15.00. The pair in the rocking chairs have toys in their laps. $15.00-20.00.

Two more pairs of Mr. and Mrs. Claus. $8.00-10.00.

These snowmen are Occupied Japan and unusual. $18.00-22.00.

Food

Corn, a popular subject for ceramics in the 1940's and 50's. There are shakers in plastic, ceramic and wood. There are corn mugs, creamers and sugars, and of course, dishes to hold the corn. These two sets are ceramic. $6.00-9.00.

Lamb chops and baked potatoes. It seems that in the 50's when so many salt and pepper clubs were popular, anything was a subject for a salt and pepper shaker. $6.00-8.00.

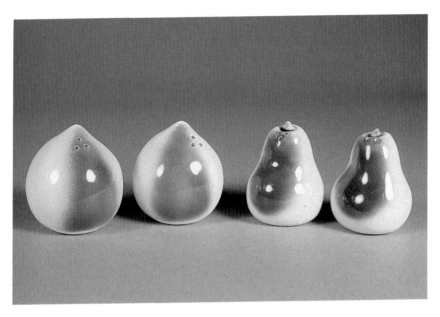

Peaches and pears. These look good enough to eat. $6.00-8.00.

Snails and clams. $6.00-8.00.

The strawberry set has four pieces–a mustard pot and a tray plus the salt and pepper. $15.00-20.00. The lemon and orange and the bananas are examples of the many kinds of fruit that appeared in the form of salt and pepper shakers. $5.00-7.00.

Crabs, clams and lobsters, all ceramic. $8.00-10.00.

Two plums on a tray. These are nicely glazed and formed. $6.00-8.00. "People fruit." There are many variations of fruit with human features, and even clothes! National Potteries Co. Cleveland, Ohio © NAPCO-Made in Japan. $25.00-30.00.

More anthropomorphic fruits and vegetables. $18.00-22.00.

Cucumbers. $6.00-8.00. Lemons & limes. $4.00-6.00. Carrot & pickle. $10.00-12.00.

Hot dogs in a bun. $8.00-10.00. Pie a la mode. The scoop of ice cream is one shaker, the pie the other. $6.00-8.00. Cupcakes with a walnut on top; chocolate and vanilla. $6.00-8.00.

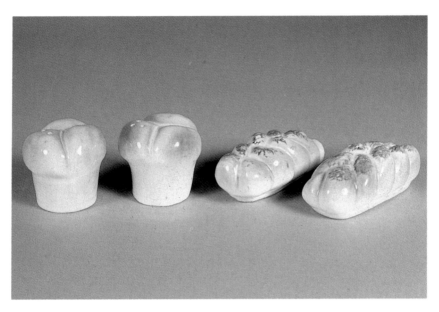

Rolls and bread. These are quite realistic looking. $6.00-8.00.

A cornucopia of fruit, and a pair of mushrooms. $4.00-6.00.

Watermelon halves and red peppers. These are luscious colors.Watermelon. $6.00-8.00. Peppers. $8.00-10.00.

Cape Cod, and what else? Lobsters. $6.00-8.00.

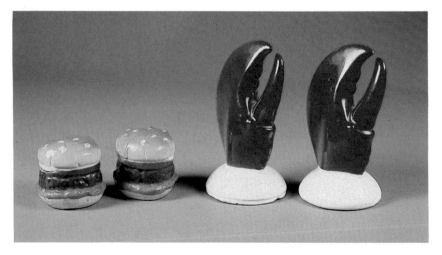

Hamburgers. These are of a chalk composition. $4.00-6.00. These lobster claws are usually large, 5½" tall. $5.00-7.00.

Kitchen Range Sets

These are range sets with nice red lettering. Since these were usually kept on the stove and used a lot the lettering is often worn. $25.00-30.00.

These were made by the Hall China Company. $30.00-35.00.

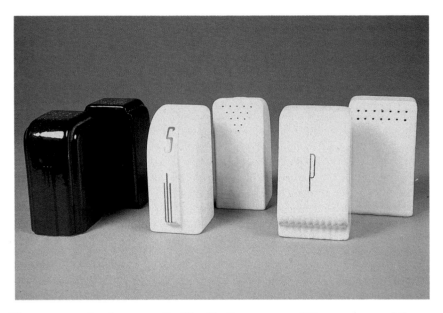

Three more sets of range salts. The black ones are a bit more unusual than the white. $25.00-30.00.

This set of range salts is Art Deco in design. $25.00-30.00.

Miniatures

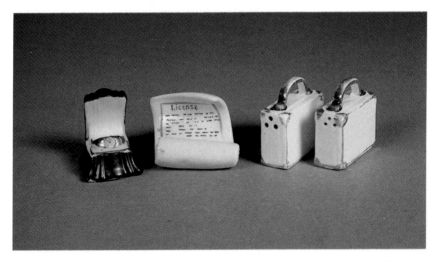

Miniatures were made to be collected, not to use as salt and pepper shakers. These two pairs are a wedding ring with a marriage license, and suitcases. $15.00-22.00.

A loaf of bread with a knife and a bar of butter on a plate with a knife. $18.00-22.00. This is a cake with a slice of it on a plate. This set is in its original package—a plastic bubble. The bottom is marked "Collectors' salt and pepper miniatures, Arcadia Ceramics, Inc. Arcadia, California." $22.00-26.00.

A spool of thread and a thimble, a school bell and McGuffey reader, and the ace of hearts and the two of clubs. $18.00-22.00.

The mail box and a package and set is a miniature; the birthday cake and present is not. The minatures measure 1" to 1½". $18.00-22.00.

Mustard Sets

This luster frog set has removable salt and pepper shakers. The mustard base is attached to the tray. $40.00-45.00.

The telephone receiver is both the salt and the pepper, one at each end. The base is a mustard pot, the dial is the removable lid. $25.00-30.00.

Toilet and potties. $8.00-10.00. Strawberry set. $10.00-15.00.

The four-piece dice set has a separate tray. $20.00-25.00. The tureens have a matching white china spoon in the mustard pot. $8.00-12.00.

The roof lifts off the middle house which is the mustard pot. These are copies of the English cottages made by Wade. They are Japanese. $15.00-20.00.

These three Dutch girls are all attached. The larger one has a spoon in her back for mustard. The heads lift out of the other two; they have long necks. This set is German, hand painted. $50.00-65.00.

Luster dog. The small dog is the pepper; the head of the larger dog lifts off and is the salt. A bright red-handled spoon (matching the ears) sits in the mustard pot body of the dog and looks like his tongue. $40.00-45.00. The fish is also luster, made in Germany, and marked "Souvenir of Montreal, Que." $40.00-45.00.

Blue and white houses. There is a mustard pot that goes with this set similar to the other house pictured. $10.00-12.00. Royal Blue mustard set. $7.00-9.00.

Nodders

Nodders have a long neck with the head resting on small notches. They fit into a base, and once set in motion, they will nod for a few minutes.

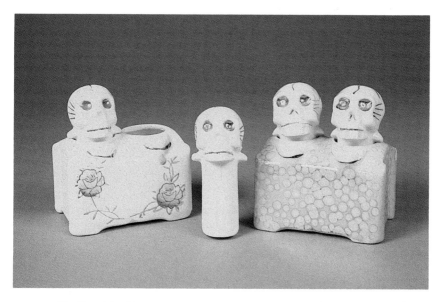

Skulls with glittering eyes and chattering teeth! $30.00-40.00.

Pigs. These are more interesting than the kind that all fit into a similar rectangular base. $115.00-125.00. The chickens are in a flower decorated base. $20.00-25.00.

The black nodder is quite rare; at least it's the first one that I've seen.
$150.00-175.00.

There are many kangaroo-baby combinations, but very few of them are nodders. This set is interesting in that the Mother's head nods from front to back,
and the baby's from side to side. $75.00-85.00. The camel base with monkeys
has a lot of detail; it is an unusual set. $150.00-175.00.

Kittens and chickens. The base shown here has been found with many different figures that are the nodders. There are sail boats and bears, pelicans and flamingos, fish and pheasants. $30.00-35.00.

Birds in a smaller base. $30.00-35.00.

Matador and Bull nodder with mustard. $75.00-85.00. Mexicans with mustard, marked "Souvenir from Mexico." $75.00-85.00.

The Indian nodders are in a base painted with an Indian motif. $25.00-30.00. Man and woman in a barrel. $50.00-75.00.

In this set the head is attached to the body with a spring. These will "nod" longer than the sets with the china notches. $25.00-30.00.

Nursery Rhyme, Fictional, and Comic Characters

The cat and the fiddle, and the cow and the moon. $18.00-20.00.

"And the dish ran away with the spoon." $18.00-20.00.

Humpty Dumpty and wall. $20.00-22.00. Jack and Jill. $20.00-22.00.

Jonah and the whale. $35.00-40.00. Old King Cole. $35.00-40.00.

Raggedy Ann and Andy (not old). $12.00-15.00.

Popeye and Olive Oyl (late 50's). $75.00-85.00.

Donkeys all dressed up. $15.00-18.00. Beatrix Potter's Peter Rabbit and Benjamin Bunny. These are Japanese, very nice. $12.00-15.00.

Howdy Doody, 1950's. $150.00-175.00. Laurel and Hardy, bone china, made by Beswick China, England. This company no longer exists as it was taken over by Doulton. The bow ties are attached to the tray. $150.00-175.00.

Paul Bunyan, axe and tree trunk. $20.00-22.00. Jack jumped over the candlestick. $20.00-22.00.

Objects: Ceramic

Pot-bellied stove and coal hod. $6.00-8.00. Pair of feet with painted red toe-nails. $6.00-8.00.

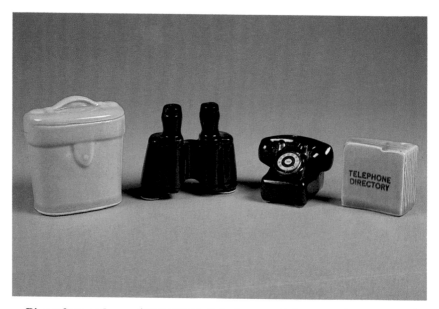

Binoculars and case. $10.00-12.00. Telephone and directory. $12.00-15.00.

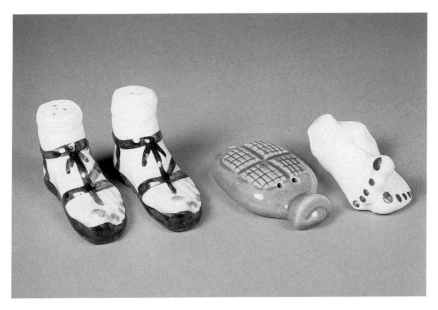

Feet in Grecian sandals. $6.00-8.00. Hot water bottle and feet. $8.00-10.00.

Record player. The arm lifts off and is one of the shakers. $12.00-15.00. Pair of suitcases. $8.00-10.00.

"Drip and Drop" in two colors. The pink ones have their name printed on their chins. $12.00-15.00.

There are many sets of beehives. The white set on the far right is Occupied Japan and is worth about 15% more than the others. $6.00-10.00.

Football and helmet; bowling ball and pin. There was certainly a salt and pepper made for everyone's interest. $8.00-10.00.

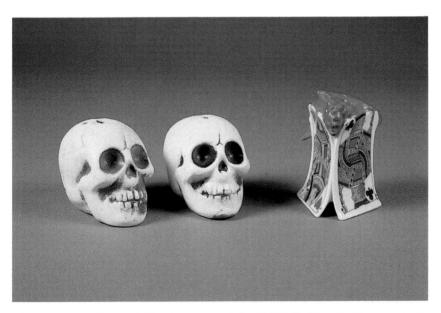

Skulls, composition chalky-type material. $6.00-9.00. The devil seems to be condemning card playing. Unfortunately, this is a single. I am curious as to what the pair might be; the same, or perhaps another vice frowned upon! Royal Bayreuth $60.00-80.00 (one). Pair $120.00-150.00.

Cigarettes and lighter; outhouse and "katalog." $10.00-15.00.

General MacArthur's hat and pipe. $18.00-22.00. Baseball mitt and ball $8.00-10.00.

These are from the 1950's, nice colors. $10.00-12.00.

Souvenir of Edison's home, Ft. Myers, FL. $8.00-10.00. Fiddle-head people.
$24.00-26.00.

Four musical instruments in wood-grained ceramic. $6.00-8.00 pair.

Pump and bucket, not particulary well formed. $6.00-8.00. Sprinkling cans, decorated. $5.00-7.00.

Pot and burner; frying pan with removable egg. $8.00-10.00.

Niagara Falls. This is a three-piece set. The falls split into two halves for the salt and pepper, and they fit on a tray. $15.00-20.00. I acquired another Niagara Falls set too late to photograph for this book. The salt is the falls; the pepper is a little boat at the base of the falls marked "Maid of the Mist." The Capitol Building and George Washington Monument are white china trimmed in gold. $12.00-15.00.

Little Red Schoolhouse and school desk. $8.00-10.00. Ink bottle and desk blotter. $6.00-8.00.

Hammer and anvil. Most of these ceramic novelty sets are from the 1950's. $6.00-8.00. Pot-bellied stove and rocker on a tray. $6.00-8.00.

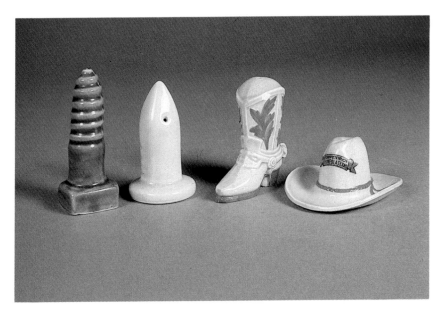

Nail and screw. $6.00-8.00. Cowboy hat and boot, souvenir of Mineola, TX. $8.00-10.00.

Gray metal tombstones read "Here lies Salt" and "Here lies Pepper." $8.00-10.00. White ceramic tombstones from Arizona (Tombstone, Arizona?) $8.00-10.00.

Shiny ceramic revolvers. $8.00-10.00.

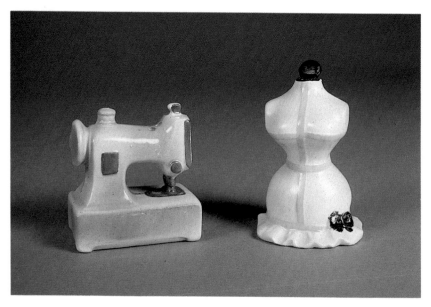

Sewing machine and dress form, marked "Lifton's exclusive U.S. pat. made in Japan." $10.00-12.00.

Scrub brush and bucket; typewriter and ink bottle. $10.00-15.00 per pair.

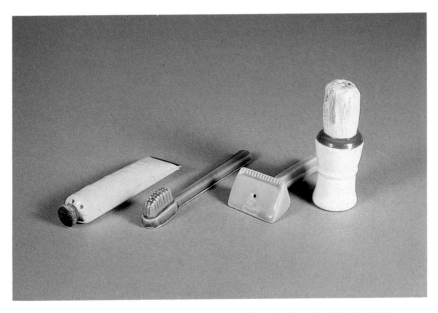

Toothbrush and toothpaste; razor and shaving brush. $10.00-15.00.

Old fashioned kitchen stove; the salt and pepper are the two pots on top. The base of the stove is for sugar. $8.00-12.00. Marked Enesco, Japan.

Fireplace and rocker. $8.00-10.00. Shoe houses. $5.00-7.00.

Golf bag and ball. $8.00-10.00. Briefcase and hat. $8.00-10.00.

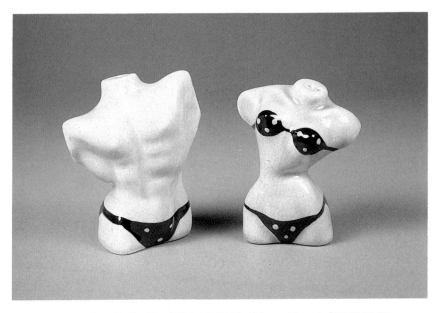

The "Yellow Polka Dot Bikini," 1950's (his and hers). $25.00-30.00.

A tiny ceramic bed and removable pillow. $8.00-10.00. A pair of legs in high-heeled shoes. $6.00-8.00.

Objects: Plastic

Plastic chefs. $8.00-10.00. Another kitchen stove, this one is plastic. $8.00-12.00. Blenders, these look like the real thing! $10.00-12.00.

Frying pans that look just like the copper bottom Revere pans that were all the rage in the 50's, but they are not marked. $5.00-7.00. The toaster without the box. $10.00-15.00.

A fairly contemporary copy of a real salt and pepper box. The pepper reads: "May cause sneezing." $10.00-12.00. Lunch box with two bottles. The stoppers come out of the bottles revealing the holes for the salt and pepper. $12.00-15.00.

A picnic table with toothpick holder and a mailbox, marked 1970. $4.00-6.00.

Champagne bucket with two bottles. They come out of the "ice" and are the salt and pepper. $15.00-20.00. A barbeque grill with two chefs, metal and plastic. $15.00-20.00.

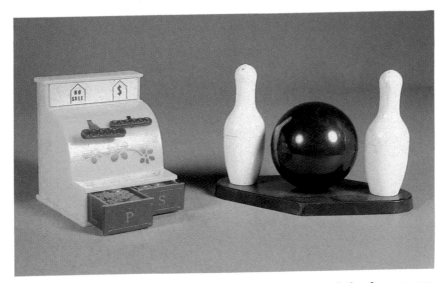

Cash register, the levers are marked salt and pepper, and the drawers are the actual shakers. $18.00-20.00. Bowling set, the bottom half of the ball is attached to the tray. The top half removes for sugar. The two pins are the shakers. $10.00-12.00.

These are miniature television sets that once were filled with "snow" (the kind you shake). $25.00-30.00.

Coffee pots. These look like chrome, but are plastic. $10.00-12.00.

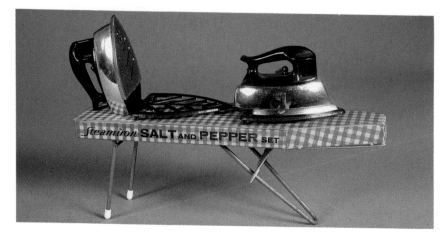

Ironing board and irons. Table legs are metal. $35.00-45.00.

Venus de Milo in black and white. $15.00-20.00. These were called "naughties" for obvious reasons. $10.00-15.00.

Toasters were, and still are, very popular. Notice the variety of colors. $8.00-12.00. In unusual colors $15.00-18.00.

These two pairs are made of Bakelite, the earliest plastic named after the man who invented it. The eggs unscrew to refill. $45.00-50.00. The birds are marked "Souvenir of Nuremberg, Germany." $45.00-50.00.

There are many wonderful shapes made in early plastic, and the colors have not faded. Many of these are geometric in shape and Art Deco in design. $15.00-22.00.

Plastic and aluminum sprinkling cans. The advertisement in the 1950 gift catalog through which so many of these were sold, says "transparent, so you can see the level of the salt." $5.00-7.00. Telephone, wall type; the bells are the salt and pepper and pop out when the crank is turned. $8.00-10.00.

This camel comes in many colors; chartreuse was popular in the 1950's. It also comes in red. $8.00-10.00. The red cats are marked salt and pepper. $4.00-6.00.

The plastic pump has a salt and pepper in the top that pops up when the pump handle is pushed. $8.00-10.00. The T.V. also has the shakers in the top and they pop up when the knob is turned. $15.00-20.00.

Ice cream sodas, strawberry and chocolate, and they look good enough to eat! Complete with straws. $8.00-10.00. The windmill blades turn from side to side, and this movement causes the shakers to pop up as shown.The windmill sits on a turquoise base which is the sugar bowl (missing from this photo). $10.00-15.00.

Bright red plastic toilets. $6.00-8.00. Guitar and music stand. $10.00-15.00.

Plastic parakeets on a branch. You really have to be a collector of plastic to love these! $8.00-10.00. A pair of binoculars to go bird watching. $6.00-8.00.

The arbor is also a napkin holder; the roses are the salt and pepper shakers. $10.00-12.00. The flower pot has the same roses as shakers. $10.00-12.00.

Objects: Metal

There are many pairs of Amish people in cast iron shakers. These are two examples. $8.00-10.00.

Amish woman milking cow. This pair has nice detail. $10.00-15.00. Locomotive and coal car; Pennsylvania Dutch type painting. $6.00-8.00.

Windmills and rocking chairs. There are also radiators, pot-bellied stoves, and various cooking utensils in this style and material. $8.00-10.00.

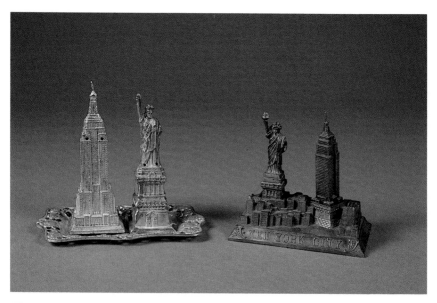

The Statue of Liberty and The Empire State Building on a rose decorated tray. 1950. $25.00-35.00. This Statue of Liberty and Empire State Building rise up out of a base that is a model of the city of New York. $35.00-45.00.

1933 Chicago Travel Building, white metal. $35.00-45.00. Boat is silvery metal and black wood and is 5" long. 1940's. $25.00-30.00.

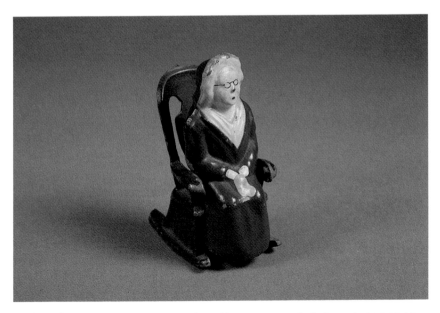

Grandma goes right off her rocker. These are metal shakers. $10.00-15.00.

A wonderful pair of cast iron Shriners, a fraternal organization that performs community service. These shakers are very realistic, almost as though they were modeled after real people. I was told by a local Shriner that there are other fraternal orders whose hat is the fez, but that only the Shriner fez is red. $85.00-100.00.

Objects: Wood

Wooden bench with a hand painted picture of St. Louis, Missouri. There are many of these benches; some have ceramic children sitting on them, but most have two holes that fit wooden shakers as shown here. $5.00-8.00. Spinning wheel. The wheel turns but doesn't "do" anything. $6.00-8.00.

A pair of pigs on a nice polished hardwood tray. $6.00-8.00. Lanterns with street signs advertising Benson Wild Animal Farm. $4.00-6.00.

A pair of dice from Bennington, VT. $6.00-8.00. Flying Saucers from Sturbridge, MA. $6.00-8.00.

Occupations

Organ grinders with monkeys. The set on the left is of better design. $15.00-18.00. The set on the right is not as good in detail. $8.00-10.00.

A Doctor and a mailman. From the 30's or 40's, these are nicely done. $20.00-25.00.

Deep-sea diver. The fish are the salt and pepper; the diver is attached to the base. $45.00-55.00.

Hard-boiled eggs. $6.00-8.00. Tom Sawyer and Becky Thatcher, characters from the Mark Twain novel. They have also appeared as lids on a canister set. The salt and pepper are 4" tall and are not marked. Part of Regal Old MacDonald farm set. $75.00-80.00.

United States presidents and wives, the Kennedys and the Johnsons. $15.00-20.00.

Sailor and fish, painted wood. $5.00-7.00. Lighthouse, Bailey Island, ME. $6.00-8.00.

Drummer and soldier are singles. $4.00-6.00 each. Maid and Bellhop. $8.00-10.00.

Horse and Jockey. $12.00-15.00. Cowboy and Horse. $12.00-15.00.

Chef and maid. $25.00-35.00. Tap dance performers. $75.00-85.00.

Pair of cowboys. $12.00-15.00. Cowboy and hat (head is one shaker, hat the other). $10.00-12.00.

These cowboys are made in Czechoslovakia. $10.00-12.00. The Cowboy on page 139 with his hat removed.

Sailors. These look like carved wood, but are of a chalk-like composition. $8.00-10.00.

Royal Canadian Mounted Police on horse. $10.00-15.00. Policeman. $6.00-8.00.

Sports figures: baseball, skiing, golf and football. $15.00-20.00 set.

Owls in doctor's clothing. $8.00-10.00. Owls in graduation garb with rhinstone eyes. $8.00-10.00.

Mailman, a single from my own collection. I keep hoping to find his mate. $4.00-6.00. Milkman, another single. I wonder if the other half of the pair is his truck or horse. The single. $15.00-25.00.

Bullfighters and bulls. These are nice ones. $8.00-10.00.

**Clowns on donkeys. $8.00-10.00. Clowns with "juicer" tops. $15.00-18.00.
Clowns standing on their hands. $15.00-18.00.**

President Kennedy in his rocking chair. $35.00-45.00. Patriotic figures. $10.00-12.00.

Two pairs of chefs. $10.00-12.00.

Chef set with mustard pot. 3½" tall. $50.00-60.00.

The two hat boxes carried by this model (stewardess, shopper?) are the salt and pepper shakers. $35.00-45.00.

Policeman and "thug." $24.00-26.00. Street cleaner, 1950. $10.00-15.00.

Angels and Devils. $6.00-8.00 pair.

Maid and cook. $6.00-8.00. Musicians. $6.00-8.00.

People

Pilgrims. $6.00-8.00. Praying girls. Part of set including cookie jar, napkin holder etc. $15.00-20.00.

Old chalkware pig heads. $8.00-10.00. Clown heads. $8.00-10.00.

These are very delicate period ladies. Note placement of shaker holes in back. $8.00-10.00. Fancy dressed women. $8.00-10.00.

Two small pairs of figural shakers. $6.00-8.00.

Dutch boy and girl, "kissing couple." $18.00-20.00. Van Tellingen "Bear Hug," one of a series of huggers. $35.00-40.00. There are dogs and a baby and a puppy. $35.00-40.00. Also a sailor and mermaid. $140.00-150.00.

Two pairs of people, origin undetermined. $6.00-8.00.

These kissing couples sit on benches, some are ceramic, some wood. These are on wooden benches. With bench, $10.00-12.00 pair.

Two charming little couples dressed in old world costumes. $8.00-10.00.

Two children sitting on a bench. $10.00-12.00. Two children who sit without a chair. These are flat on the bottom and will sit on floor or table. The others will not balance without a bench or chair. These children are reading. $8.00-12.00.

Woman with rolling pin and husband in the dog house, a very popular theme of the 1950's. Marked "Vallona Starr, Vallona, Ca." $60.00-75.00. Two slices of pie. $6.00-8.00.

A pair of ladies' heads, reminiscent of Betty Boop. $18.00-22.00. An interesting pair, more finely sculted than some. $12.00-15.00.

This bride and groom is Occupied Japan. $15.00-20.00. Stork carrying a baby (what else?) $15.00-18.00.

The bride and groom on the left are part of a group of two-sided people. On this side, "before" is printed. $18.00-22.00. The small bride was made by Goebel in 1951, and designed by Carl Wagner. The salt and pepper shakers were part of a line of functional pieces, including creamers and sugars. The groom is not marked, and although I bought them as a pair, the groom is not Goebel. The bride has the bee in V mark, and the serial number is impressed. Bride and groom. $65.00-80.00.

The reverse or "after" side of the bride and groom. The bride is pregnant, and the husband has a paunch. The train on the Goebel bride is nicely textured.

This two-sided couple are happy in this view, and the bride and groom are young and handsome. $18.00-22.00.

On the reverse side, the happy couple are angry, and the bride and groom are middle-aged.

A pair of hillbillies taking a snooze. $8.00-10.00. A hillbilly with a "moonshine" jug. $8.00-10.00.

People of Different Nationalities

Indians. These are very collectible. $6.00-8.00.

The seated Indians are older than the preceeding pairs. $8.00-10.00. Indian
with tom-tom. $12.00-15.00.

These Indians are of wood-grained ceramic. $5.00-7.00. Indian heads. $6.00-8.00.

The Indian's arms form a circle, so he can perch on the tepee. $25.00-35.00. Pair of Indian children (cartoon type). $6.00-8.00.

Two more sets of Indian shakers. $8.00-10.00.

This Indian head is nicely detailed and is more realistic than most sets. The totem pole makes the pair. $10.00-12.00.

Kachina dolls. The Kachina is an ancestral spirit deified by the Hopi Indians of northern Arizona. They were impersonated in religious festivals by masked dancers. There are many 20th century souvenirs of the Kachina dolls. These salt and pepper shakers are decorated with real feathers. $15.00-18.00.

In the pair on the left, both the Indian and the canoe are the shakers. $10.00-12.00. Both Indians in the set on the right are the shakers. There is a mustard pot between them. $15.00-18.00.

Hugging Eskimos. $8.00-10.00. Two Eskimos in a canoe. $10.00-12.00.

The stereotype of the Mexican taking a siesta with or without cactus abounds in salt and pepper shakers. Seated Mexicans. $8.00-10.00. Two figures on tray with cactus. $5.00-7.00.

Two pairs of cactus. (I actually met someone who collected only cactus sets). $5.00-7.00 pair. Mexican couple is Occupied Japan. $10.00-15.00.

Eastern man seated on pillow. $12.00-15.00. Eastern woman with "mosque." $12.00-15.00.

Oriental couple. $8.00-10.00. Oriental heads. $8.00-10.00. Pagodas. $10.00-12.00.

Oriental girl with teahouse. $12.00-15.00. Oriental couple. It seems odd that man is full figured and woman is only half. Color and glaze is identical on both, so I am sure that they are a pair. $15.00-18.00.

The United States

In the 1950's and 60's, states and their symbols were sold through Heather House in Burlington, IA, for $1.25 a pair. All inquiries that I made to this and other mail order companies were returned to me, address unknown. Through a friend, I was able to copy the list of states and their symbols from the original catalog. It is easy to pass up the mate to one of the states; without the list, it is impossible to guess what would pair up with each state. I am reprinting it here for the convenience of collectors. I was also fortunate to receive marvelous slides of a map collage assembled by John Fawcett, a Professor of Art at the University of Connecticut. The collage is owned by Noel and Lynn Barrett, proprietors of Rosebud Antiques of Carversville, Pennsylvania. I am so grateful to Mr. Barrett for taking the photograph and allowing me to reproduce it in this book.

"The 38 United States of America" from the private collection of Noel and Lynn Barrett. Not for sale.

Vermont and syrup bucket; Massachusetts and bean pot. All states $22.00-24.00.

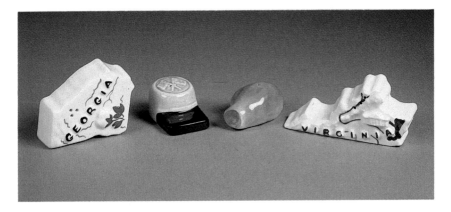

Georgia and Confederate cap: Virginia and ham. $22.00-24.00.

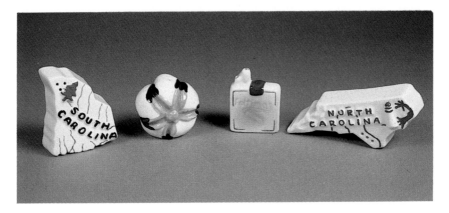

South Carolina and cotton; North Carolina and cigarettes. $22.00-24.00.

Oklahoma and Indian; Nevada and the ace of spades. $22.00-24.00.

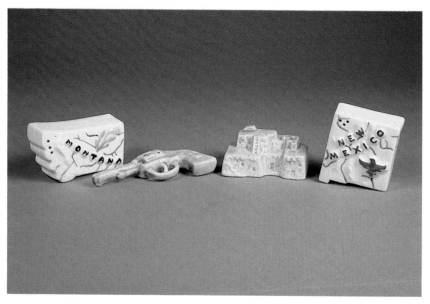

Montana and gun; New Mexico and pueblo. $22.00-24.00.

Arizona and cactus; Wyoming and bronco. $22.00-24.00.

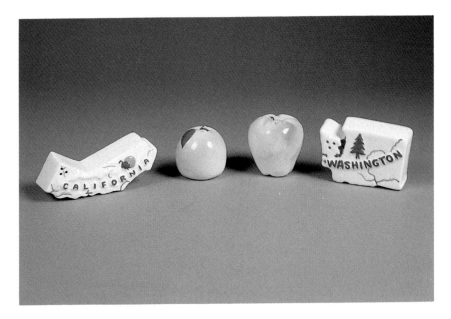

California and orange; Washington and apple. $22.00-24.00.

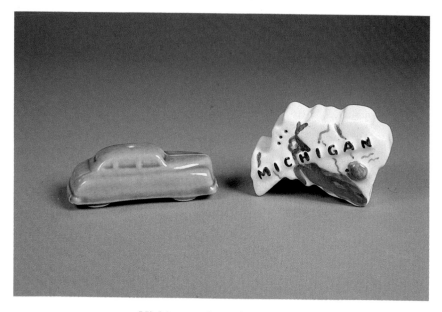

Michigan and car. $22.00-24.00.

New York and the Statue of Liberty; New Jersey and Miss America. $22.00-24.00.

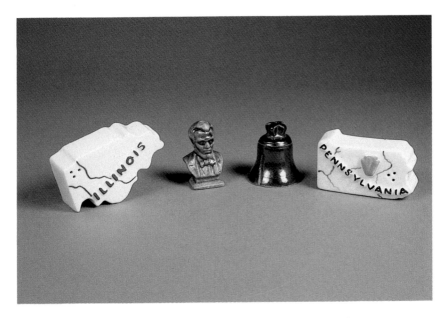

Illinois and Lincoln; Pennsylvania and the Liberty Bell. $22.00-24.00.

Wisconsin and cheese; West Virginia and coal. $22.00-24.00.

Rhode Island and rooster; Connecticut and graduation cap. $22.00-24.00.

Hawaii and native girl; Alaska and igloo. $22.00-24.00.

The prices for the state sets are per pair. Supply and demand, however, would affect the price. They can still be found for less than $6.00, but if a collector needed certain ones to complete the set of 50, he would probably pay more than the going price. Here is the complete list:

Alaska and igloo
Alabama and watermelon
Arizona and cactus
Arkansas and razorback
California and orange
Colorado and pack mule
Connecticut and graduation cap
Delaware and lighthouse
Florida and fish
Georgia and Confederate cap
Hawaii and native girl
Idaho and potato
Illinois and Lincoln
Indiana and racer
Iowa and corn
Kansas and wheat
Kentucky and jug
Louisiana and sugar sack
Maine and pine tree
Maryland and oyster
Massachusetts and bean pot
Michigan and car
Minnesota and canoe

Montana and six shooter
Nebraska and cowboy boot
Nevada and ace of spades
New Hampshire and snowman
New Jersey and Miss America
New Mexico and pueblo
New York and Statue of Liberty
North Carolina and cigarettes
North Dakota and oil well
Ohio and tire
Oklahoma and Indian
Oregon and duck
Pennsylvania and Liberty Bell
Rhode Island and rooster
South Carolina and cotton
South Dakota and pheasant
Tennessee and horse head
Texas and cowboy hat
Utah and covered wagon
Vermont and maple syrup bucket
Virginia and ham
Washington and apple
West Virginia and coal

The American flags were made by the same company and may have accompanied the States. $24.00-28.00.

Transportation

Ceramic locomotive and coal car. $8.00-10.00. Stagecoaches. $8.00-10.00.

1950's car (complete with fins) driven by two serious dogs. The trunk lid comes off and reveals a mustard pot. $30.00-40.00.

Plastic boat on which the smokestacks are the salt and pepper. $6.00-8.00.
Trailer truck; cab has a notch to connect the trailer. $12.00-15.00.

Bronze steam engines. $6.00-8.00. All metal, tray with tunnel, marked "New
Jersey Turnpike." The salt and pepper are shiny old fashioned cars. $18.00-
22.00.

This single I call "taxi-lady." I would love to know what piece paired with her-another person, or perhaps, a yellow checkered cab. If anyone knows, I'd like to hear about it. $18.00 (two alike, pair $60.00-70.00). Dog and car are the shakers; steering wheel is attached to dog. $18.00-22.00.

Boy and girl sitting on boats. $18.00-22.00. Sailor lying in boat. $26.00-28.00.

Conestoga wagon and pioneer, ceramic. $6.00-8.00. Wooden conestoga wagons, souvenir of Green Mts., VT. $4.00-6.00.

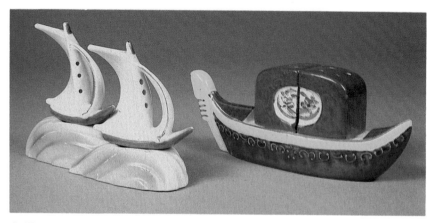

Sailboat in a wave. Note placement of holes on the mast. Gondola, many of these are decorated with peoples' names. $12.00-15.00.

Old fashioned cars, marked "S.D.D. copyright 1931." $7.00-9.00. Plastic, old-fashioned car with people as shakers. $12.00-15.00.

Metal tricycle with glass salt and pepper shakers. $12.00-16.00.

Racing cars, sticker reads "Rolling Racing car salt and pepper; Authentic Mercedes Benz." Japan. $12.00-18.00. Wooden cars are 2" tall, and are 40-50 years old. The wheels roll. $10.00-15.00.